Circadian Motherhood

Elsa Barnhill

Presentation by *BookLeaf Publishing*

Web: www.bookleafpub.com

E-mail: info@bookleafpub.com

ISBN: 9789358368086

First edition 2023

To my daughters, who both inspire and restrain me, and to God who gave me the privilege of raising them.

AUBADE, AS A SOLO

When calm over takes the squeals of the day
I join the victory, wearing my shoes

The loud zippers can be quiet at night
vulgar shades of rouge are mute in low light
perfume spritzes can be hidden simply-
in the always present bathroom dirt cloud

Mother's guilt can hide in remnants of youth

Now, complete with anti-battle dressing
I'll drink and dabble in blurred up moments
By not remembering my real self
Believing just what I look like

Caressing myself with uncounted hours
Sweet talking myself with profane phrases
Holding myself to the promise I've had
Loving myself as I existed before

Then when the return beacon lights the day
It will quickly draw me, and guilt, back home
To spend another day as almost me,
but also extra me
So stay dark sky and let me be.

WILDGIRLS

Lying in a dusky bedroom
One breast out
Containing my rage
Waiting on stillness
To mark my escape anytime now

I've done this before,
Two or three times
Then the pain is gone
Quick as it came
But knowing this doesn't change me

One day I'll wake and sun will light the room
before my anger does
I'll rise tepidly and stop torturing the carpet with
my toes
The ones wishing for prudence, polish, and
plush slippers

That day I'll taste new coffee
Not jagged words
Injuring gentle spirits
Of waiting wildgirls
And join them in the pink plastic wilderness

I'll want to sit beside them
Collecting waxy rainbows
Healing their wounds
Not pretend smiling
Their laughs actually appeasing me

I'll stop memory gambling wondering if they
will remember
Decorated birthdays or undeserved disgraces
Or if those times were good, bad or neutral

For now, I'll head back to rooms and wait
Without a cry
Or need for breast
To watch a
Tiny breathing chest

NEON-LIT OBSERVATIONS

Why do drops always fall on steering wheel bottoms
not pooling into salty lakes
and why do my busy hands not object
and erase them with a smear?

I notice them while sitting in fluorescent parking lots
Paying a liquid price to speak with a deity
using a funny currency exchange of
asking to trade miracles for good behavior

Now this rinsed steering wheel
is dry and ready for the next session
my cheeks wiped and ready too
hiding my little indiscretion

The garage door opens loudly
Quiet steps and light soul
More items than I left with
But carrying less than before

WHEN I STAND BY A SPRINGTIME POOL

When I stand by a springtime pool
on steaming concrete
in the straw hat
my sister left last summer,
with the teal stripe,
I'm not staring at the water
that keeps splashing on my toes
but at your picture on the surface,
the one of tiny kids playing
that I don't get to keep

EN TU CUERO LO HALLARÁS

En tu cuero lo hallarás.
You will find it in your skin, she always told me

What, I thought, will I find except
palor, freckles, and wiry spikes embarrassing me with
their lack of delicacy
but now it's become clear
Now that I repeat it daily

when fear-churned wonder demands a finger on
red-hot or
feet clamor to climb air
once the hot iron singes and little legs beat the ground
their skin, the thin and new one, finds it

Its in the empty space that cries for comfort
But only whispers pride
Its in the beggy-bragging while climbing the top bar
And in the black-top bruises that are born of it

Where the need is to be a baby
but the desire of being free is even bigger
and I am forced to allow it
but not without saying
En tu cuero lo hallarás.

CHEERS TO US BOTH

When I watch you succeed at
something
I succeed a little too

Sit and listen for a moment

Though the victory is never mine
and I would never take it,
the breaths
the dance-beat heart
the ignored scratch on your calf
the urge to find your sister
the pinch of your left shoe
the scowl of your teacher-coach
the telepathic begging for approval,

I wanted to take those
To take them all from you
But I didn't
and you felt them

I only felt them as a double
in the haunting way a mother pretends
is the same as your way

That's the way we share success
and now, my darling, you may go back to sleep

DELAY

What was your biggest childhood fear?

First let me finish this page

What makes the moon come up at night?

Now I have to read it over again

Did you always want a daughter?

I thought this was your favorite book?

Were you mad when I quit dance class?

The one with monkeys that get stuck?

Why do I have to learn another language?

Ok, let me put this down.

I'll never learn to do a backflip.

We are past your bedtime now.

What's that breathy sound you always make?

Ok, I'll tell you everything-
You see, my biggest fear in childhood
Was being too lonely at night

I can see you feel it too, though now you're not
even awake

REVERSE ALCHEMY

Look at you go,
You fantastic independent machine!
Why, it was only yesterday
that your water cup sat empty
from my personal neglect

Look at you now,
Banana globs on your arms
Gloating at your command of cracking eggs
So gently into bowls
But with ungentle eyebrows

Look at your potential!
You are willing to barter childhood sloth for
batter!
But are we so sure
now is the time
to make that trade?

PROJECTIONS

Here we are!
twirl chasing each other
at the star room,
finally together,
plagiarizing each other's
smiles and movements

Who would have known
I was just scowling
at your compatriots,
innocence be damned,
for rejecting you
thereby rejecting me?

Here we go again!
Staring at the real
technicolor heavens
and forgetting our place
our true place
under them

Who would have known
that we were just
saying that we never see
real things,

Just projections?
And now projections of real things
are just what we needed

Here, we are moving-
you would know it-
if you saw us dance for ourselves now
in this very real place,
a place where we did not reject ourselves

URGENT CARE

14

Why are you mad?
But I'm not mad.
It's only the tattoo
I got the day
you tore your chin
when I wanted to keep
wandering at the botanical garden's
October show
The flairs were added
when I yelled at
everyone for crying
and making it all about yourself
but once all was sown together
I thought,
I can't have anything
any thing
at all.

SUNFLOWERS

I'm trying to duplicate
the story I heard
about sunflowers
being a solitary bright spot
in an otherwise solitary sad time

The way a mother
teaches you to love
colored glass bottles
I wanted to teach you
to love a garden

to remember grass instead of dirt
and sunflowers purposely planted
once on the edges
even if I only bother once
to do it right

Tending to annuals
in childhood homes
is not different from
tending to memories
afterall

SOUNDS OF SEVEN

Pixel pixel pix elle
an ice pop in the summer sun
is perfect
and the dancing during
questions confuses
but delights me
in the middle of the day

La la la la lava
at night while I am
trying to write
keeps trying my patience
but also forming
la la lovely notes
for end of day

loud little pixie
why are you
allowed to scream
when I was not?
But in my hands now,
though the loud disquiets me,
I will not dis quiet you

NOTHING IS WORSE

17

Nothing is worse than that mother
that does nothing.

Her kids, like progress,
pollute the air with their cries.

Nothing is worse than that mother
that does nothing

to understand our pristine frustrations and wont
give soothing to our cries.

THERE MUST BE POISON
IN MY COFFEE

There must be poison in my coffee.

This morning when you woke up
and asked me what
I would make for dinner

and rubbed your owlette
eyes without the
dark circles under them

I wanted to cradle
your sleepy fresh face
and let you take my blanket

but listening to your dream,
about parties in a car,
inspired me not to drink it

because it was at that moment
with a heart full
of cheap lemon grace

I figured out
shocking!
My daily mistake

It starts out so easy
the sweet give and take
of the day

but moving along.
once I take a sip,
the bitterness pours out on its own

ARBITRATION

Bring me your anger
Little masters of destruction
Bring me all of it
The bits you left outside
Glistening in the late day sun

Put it all in my hands
The ones I use to lift you
For only I can turn off
its toxic air effects
And somehow save us all

Let me put it in my basket
I think we left a little space
From the last time
The poison reared its ugly face

I can't help but laugh as
You look at me in awe now
haven't you noticed
I need it back because it came from me?

THE END AND THE BEGINNING

I sent defeat to school one morning
It wasn't hard to wake it
As it was tired of laying low
I packed it's bag of judgment and despair due tomorrow
And dressed it in complacency

I fed it one last meal of insecurity
And urged it to come quick with me
Until it left the place it paced around at night
Eager to grow and couldn't know
It would never come back home

I stayed with it, while it persistently pursued me
Until the bell rang.
One last time we said goodbye
in the same way you say goodbye
to a friend you never liked

Now the drive home
is without a part two
and white flags will not color
my 2:42
we finally have space for a victory

TIME AND TIME AGAIN

It is said that the days beginning and end
Is marked by the sun's graph across the sky

but my house of cards and children
is run by numberlight not sky
beginning at late number time
and continued
by darkened toast 1-5,
depending on your preference.

It follows then
channel ten point one
for at least five more minutes
and if I have to ask you one more time
and i've already seen you twice
completes the afternoon

numbers haunting us at dinner
three more bites
and one forbidden word
which bring the angry countdowns
to both punishment and future pleasure
when the numbers finally stop

its barely have a breath a clock
and I am sitting in the dark

MERCY

We once hated a rabbit,
though you'll deny it soon enough,

but I taught you to hate it and
hate it you did.

The way it quick-consumed
multi day flower work

The way it made your pattern mother frown
and took an edge to yesterdays delight

But I can still see your confusion
when I looked at you with dread

that day you ran over triumphantly
to tell me it was dead

But have you forgotten? Just last year
you plucked my four-leafed sprouts
on the 17th of March.

Let it be known:
my green intentions were planted in the wrong place.
But lucky me, it's quick, when mercy germinates.

YOUR PICTURE ON INDEPENDENCE DAY

When I go back to it and visit you,
cherry popsicled and silly smiling
from convention breaking sugar
I can almost feel the lightness of
the white woven smock
Covering your bony sun-printed shoulders
and draping beauty so intense that I could cry

And not to mention,
your crown of orderly bangs
Framing mischievous eyes
That sparkled!
Sparkled next to sparklers
That you wanted
But I cowardly withheld

In their place you held up
A golden corn dog
and daddys phone in your crooked arm,
you daughter of an immigrant!
A perfect pose before the flash
A statuette of liberty
just yearning to breathe free

www.ingramcontent.com/pod-product-compliance
Lightning Source LLC
La Vergne TN
LVHW010854200726
843508LV00012B/2892